ANOTHER BEAD,
ANOTHER PRAYER

ANOTHER BEAD, ANOTHER PRAYER

DEVOTIONS TO USE
with Protestant Prayer Beads

KRISTEN E. VINCENT
and
MAX O. VINCENT

UPPER
ROOM BOOKS®
NASHVILLE

ANOTHER BEAD, ANOTHER PRAYER
Devotions to Use with Protestant Prayer Beads
© 2014 by Kristen E. Vincent and Max O. Vincent.
All rights reserved.

Upper Room Books® website: books.upperroom.org
Cover design: Bruce Gore | GoreStudio.com
Cover photo: Kristen E. Vincent
Bead instruction photos: Blanka Gresham
Author photo: Gerald Patrick Photography

At the time of publication all websites referenced in this book were valid. However, due to the fluid nature of the internet some addresses may have changed, or the content may no longer be relevant.

Scripture quotations not otherwise identified are from the Common English Bible. Copyright © 2011 Common English Bible. Used by permission.

Scripture passages designated NRSV are taken from the New Revised Standard Version Bible © 1989, Division of Christian Education of the National Council of the Churches of Christ in the United States of America. Used by permission. All rights reserved.

Brief excerpts are taken from *The New Interpreter's Dictionary of the Bible* (Nashville, TN: Abingdon Press, 2009), volume and page cited in text.

LIBRARY OF CONGRESS CATALOGING-IN-PUBLICATION DATA
Vincent, Kristen E.
  Another bead, another prayer : devotions to use with Protestant prayer beads / Kristen E. Vincent and Max O. Vincent.
      pages cm
  ISBN 978-0-8358-1372-3 (print) — ISBN 978-0-8358-1373-0 (mobi) — ISBN 978-0-8358-1374-7
1. Prayer—Christianity. 2. Beads—Religious aspects—Christianity. 3. Prayers. I. Title.

  BV227.V56 2015
  242'.8—dc23

                                                          2014030544

Printed in the United States of America

To

MATTHEW ISAAC

You are indeed God's gift of laughter.

We learn so much from you

in trying to teach you how to pray.

CONTENTS

ACKNOWLEDGMENTS

THANKS TO THE STAFF of Upper Room Books for their continued support, encouragement, and professionalism. Your publications reveal your attention to detail and your deep faith.

Thanks to the staff of Square Perk Cafe in Covington, Georgia, where we wrote much of this book. We appreciate your letting us camp out in your booths while feeding us with caffeine, good food, and warm hearts.

As always, our son, Matthew, sustains us in all of our work with his love, quick wit, and an understanding of God's love that is beyond his years. We often play a game where we try to one-up each other on the depth of our love. "I love you to the moon and back," we will say. "Well, I love you to the stars and back times a million," he replies. One day we told him we loved him "to God and back," believing that trumped anything else. Without missing a beat he retorted, "That's not very far because God is right here with us." Indeed. We love you, Matthew, infinity times infinity.

So too we love God to infinity times infinity. And we thank God for this book and all that it represents. Our hope for you is that these prayers will help you grow in God's infinite love.

INTRODUCTION

MY HUSBAND AND I were awed by the response to *A Bead and a Prayer: A Beginner's Guide to Protestant Prayer Beads*. We received countless testimonies from people who have turned—or re-turned—to God and the church, developed a greater comfort level with prayer, and experienced a deeper connection with the Lord. Our readers received news of the gift of praying with beads in the manner we intended: with love. For that we are deeply grateful.

Along with testimonies, we received numerous requests for a follow-up book, one that would provide additional devotions. The first book whetted readers' appetites, and they hungered for more ways to use Protestant prayer beads. I knew immediately that I wanted to write this collection; creating new prayer bead devotions is one of my great loves. I also knew I wanted to collaborate with my husband, Max. He served as my principal theological adviser on the first book; it made sense

11

to coauthor the second with him. And so, together we offer this collection of prayers.

HOLY, HOLY, HOLY

We draw our inspiration for this collection from Isaiah 6:3-5. The prophet describes a vision in which he encounters the Lord. The encounter begins with praise as winged creatures shout, "Holy, holy, holy is the LORD of heavenly forces! All the earth is filled with God's glory!" Recognizing God's greatness, Isaiah confronts his own limitations. He responds with confession: "Mourn for me; I'm ruined! I'm a man with unclean lips." He then takes the opportunity to intercede—to lift up his prayer concerns—for his community: "I live among a people with unclean lips." As God receives Isaiah's confession and petitions, the prophet thanks the Lord for God's graciousness: "Yet I've seen the king, the LORD of heavenly forces!"

Isaiah's encounter with God provides a wonderful model for prayer. Consider this: You stand face-to-face with God, the Creator of all things and the one who embodies love. What would you do? It seems natural that you would begin with praise (once the shock and awe wears off enough for you to be able to speak!).

From there you might offer apologies for your short-comings before sharing the needs and concerns of your heart. Still, as you sit in the presence of love, your heart and mind would fill with the innumerable ways in which God has acted in your life, inspiring an ever-flowing litany of thanks and praise. Praise, confession, intercession, thanksgiving; these four types of prayer found in this scene from Isaiah form the four collections of prayers in this book. We will return to this scene at the start of each section to begin our prayers.

Another way of looking at it is this: Praise is about God's relationship with creation, while thanksgiving is about God's relationship with us as humans. Confession is about our relationship with God, just as intercession describes our relationship with creation. Since God is the Alpha and the Omega, the beginning and the end, our relationships and the prayers that result naturally fit within the context of God. A circular progression flows naturally:

DEVOTION AND MEDITATION

These four forms of prayer provide the structure for the prayers, all of which are based on scripture. Each prayer is comprised of

1. a complete devotion in which God calls us to connect with God, and we respond, and
2. a listening meditation in which we call out to God, and God faithfully responds.

In other words, the devotion helps us focus on the words that we have to offer to God, while the meditation enables us to listen to what God has to say to us.

We offer many differing prayers for use with your beads. You need not use the prayers in the order they appear unless you find that approach meaningful. So too you may choose to use the devotion and not the meditation, or vice versa. You may want to use the same prayer over the course of days or weeks, or you may want to choose a new one daily. Feel free to use what fits your mood or place in life.

Also note that you do not need to recite each devotion word for word. These are not scripts; you do not need to hold the book while using your beads. It is better that your hands and mind are free to relax and follow the path of the beads. Read over a prayer to get the general idea of its purpose. Then sit back, relax, and pray in your own words. Indeed, we encourage you to write your own devotions or meditations at some point and have included a guide in the back of the book to help with this. Our greatest hope is for you to grow in your experience of prayer.

We do not assume that you are familiar with the content of *A Bead and a Prayer: A Beginner's Guide to Protestant Prayer Beads.* You will find background information on Protestant prayer beads in the following section. At the back of the book a Leader's Guide offers a variety of uses for this book. You will also find instructions for making prayer beads as well as resources for purchasing supplies.

God calls us into a relationship filled with God's deep love. We invite you to take up your beads and respond with words from the heart.

PROTESTANT PRAYER BEADS

Welcome! You are embarking on a journey that will introduce you to a new way of connecting with God. Protestant prayer beads are a prayer tool that can help you experience God's presence, increase your focus and comfort level in prayer, and be still and know God's love for you.

While many types of prayer beads exist, we designed the devotions and meditations in this book for use with Protestant prayer beads. Many Protestants are unfamiliar with this form of prayer beads; they are generally more familiar with the beads used by Catholics to pray the rosary. The two forms of prayer beads certainly have some common history, evolving as a way for Christians to "pray continually" (1 Thess. 5:17). The rosary is at least one thousand years old, but a group of Episcopalians in Texas developed Protestant prayer beads in the 1980s. The group wanted to reclaim ancient prayer practices, and after meeting for a period of time they created the "Anglican rosary," a format of prayer beads for Protestant use.

Sixty beads make up the rosary; Protestant prayer beads are made up of a cross or other pendant and thirty-three or more beads. One large bead, called the "invitatory" bead, reminds us that God invites us to a time of prayer. We use this bead to begin our prayer, much like churches employ a call to worship to begin a church service.

In addition to the large invitatory bead, we find four more large beads. When we splay out a set of Protestant prayer beads, these beads form the four points of a cross and thus are called "cruciform" beads. Beyond representing the points of the cross, the number 4 reminds us of the four Gospels, the four seasons of the year, the four parts of our day (morning, afternoon, evening, and night), and the four directions (north, south, east, and west).

Between each of the cruciform beads is a set of seven smaller beads. Because a week has seven days, these beads are called "week" beads. Like the number 4, the number 7 has bountiful meaning for Christians:

- The church calendar consists of seven seasons (Advent, Christmas, Epiphany, Lent, Easter, Pentecost, and Ordinary Time).

- Genesis tells us there were seven days of creation; on the seventh day God rested, calling us to keep it holy;
- the number 7 shows up often in the book of Revelation, including John's note that his letter is addressed to the "seven churches" (1:4);
- both Jews and Christians believe the number 7 symbolizes spiritual perfection.

When we add together the one invitatory bead, the four cruciform beads, and the twenty-eight week beads, we get a total of thirty-three beads. (See diagram on page 21.) The group that developed this format appreciated this number since it represented Jesus' life on earth for thirty-three years.

As Kristen explained in *A Bead and a Prayer*, for the first year she chose to use that number of beads. However, over time she began to desire some representation of the fact that Christ still lives today, particularly since the Resurrection is the hallmark of the Christian faith. So she added one more bead, positioning it between the invitatory bead and the bottom cruciform bead. She calls it the "resurrection" bead and uses it in her prayers to focus on Christ's gift to us of eternal life. Adding this bead makes the total number of beads thirty-four. However, she still tells people that Protestant prayer beads are comprised of thirty-three beads, which represent Jesus' life and ministry on earth—plus one bead to represent his resurrection.

We want to emphasize that there is no right or wrong way to make your prayer beads. This study will focus on the Protestant prayer bead format of thirty-four beads; however, you may design your own format as we did and modify the devotions accordingly. Since this is your prayer tool, it should be meaningful for you and your time with the Lord.

Like the rosary, Protestant prayer beads offer various benefits to prayer: They enhance focus, offer a way of being still, and serve as a sign of God's presence. But whereas the rosary has a formula for prayers to be said with each bead, Protestant prayer beads do not. This means you can use them in any way that feels comfortable to you and even experiment with different ways of using them, depending upon your need at the time. Consider this a wonderful opportunity to explore new ways of being with God.

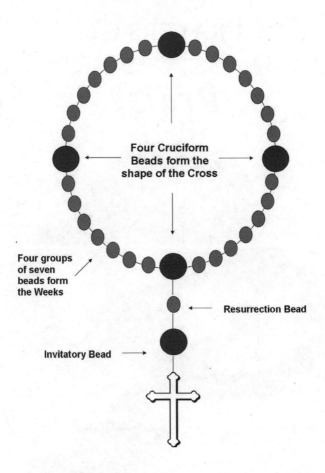

Four Cruciform
Beads form the
shape of the Cross

Four groups
of seven
beads form
the Weeks

Resurrection Bead

Invitatory Bead

PRAYERS OF

Praise

WHO GOD IS IN RELATION TO CREATION

From the opening chapters of Genesis where God speaks creation into being to the closing pages of Revelation where God comes to dwell among us, the Bible bears witness to God's acting in time and space. Praise is our witness and recognition of God's presence in our midst. *The New Interpreter's Dictionary of the Bible* says, "Praise is motivated by gratitude for God's actions in the world (especially the more expansive ones), wonder and awe at God's qualities of creativeness, justice, and everlasting love, and joy over God's saving actions" (vol. 4, 578).

Praise involves seeing ourselves and our world as part of God's creation. It acknowledges who God is in relation to the world around us. We have chosen seven passages to communicate the various expressions of praise we encounter in scripture. Use the following prayers and meditations to express the gratitude, awe, and joy that lie at the heart of the biblical concept of praise.

PRAISING GOD'S GLORY

> Winged creatures were stationed around him. Each had six wings: with two they veiled their faces, with two their feet, and with two they flew about. They shouted to each other, saying: "Holy, holy, holy is the LORD of heavenly forces! All the earth is filled with God's glory! The doorframe shook at the sound of their shouting, and the house was filled with smoke.
>
> —ISAIAH 6:2–4

Isaiah's vision of God begins with the praise of the angels around God's throne. Witnessing praise invites us to join in praise. The devotion invites us to see our praise of God in union with the praise of the angels that Isaiah witnessed. The meditation focuses on the hymn of holiness the angels sing.

Devotion

Cross: Holy God, heaven and earth are filled with your glory.

Invitatory bead: Let my praise be united with that of the angels as we proclaim that

Resurrection bead: you are holy, holy, holy. Amen.

1st cruciform bead: Lord, you sit enthroned on the praises of the angels.

24

Week beads, set 1: Use each bead to listen to the praises of the angels.

2nd cruciform bead: God of light, I bow with the angels before your glory.

Week beads, set 2: Use each bead to show reverence to God.

3rd cruciform bead: God of holiness, I join my voice with the praise of the angels.

Week beads, set 3: Use each bead to join with the angels in praising God.

4th cruciform bead: Mighty God, let the earth shake with the sound of my praise.

Week beads, set 4: Use each bead to listen to the earth as it shakes from the sound of your praise.

Resurrection bead: Glory be to you,

Invitatory bead: Father, Son, and Holy Spirit,

Cross: one God forever and ever, filling the earth with your glory.

Meditation

With each bead: Lord, you are holy, holy, holy.

PRAISING THE GOD OF CREATION

When I look up at your skies, at what your fingers made—the moon and the stars that you set firmly in place—what are human beings that you think about them; what are human beings that you pay attention to them?

—PSALM 8:3-4

Psalm 8 celebrates the place of human beings within all creation. The psalmist expresses wonder and amazement at the majesty and vastness of creation. Then he marvels at the unique relationship God holds with humans among the cosmos. The devotion uses the "Gloria Patri" and other words from the full text of Psalm 8, including the title "Lord" to address God. The meditation invites us to consider the psalmist's question, "What are human beings that you pay attention to them?" Use the meditation as a way of listening for God's answer.

Devotion

Cross: Glory be to the Father and to the Son and to the Holy Spirit;

Invitatory bead: as it was in the beginning, is now, and ever shall be,

Resurrection bead: world without end. Amen.

1ˢᵗ cruciform bead: Lord, you set lights in the heavens for the day and the night.

Week beads, set 1: Use each bead to express awe for the sun and moon, the planets and stars.

2ⁿᵈ cruciform bead: Lord, you created the earth and filled it with living things.

Week beads, set 2: Use each bead to express a sense of wonder for all living things.

3ʳᵈ cruciform bead: Creator God, you have formed humans out of the dust of the earth.

Week beads, set 3: Use each bead to express wonder at the human body as a creation.

4ᵗʰ cruciform bead: You have created me to be in relationship with you.

Week beads, set 4: Use each bead to praise God for the different ways you can relate to God in the midst of creation.

Resurrection bead: Glory be to the Father and to the Son and to the Holy Spirit;

Invitatory bead: as it was in the beginning, is now, and ever shall be,

Cross: world without end. Amen.

Meditation

With each bead: "What am I?"

Praising with Your Whole Being

> Praise the LORD! Praise God in his sanctuary! Praise God in his fortress, the sky! / Praise God in his mighty acts! Praise God as suits his incredible greatness! / Praise God with the blast of the ram's horn! Praise God with lute and lyre! / Praise God with drum and dance! Praise God with strings and pipe! / Praise God with loud cymbals! Praise God with clashing cymbals! / Let every living thing praise the LORD! Praise the LORD!

—PSALM 150

Psalm 150 invites earth and heaven, sanctuary and sky, to unite in praise to God. It encourages us to employ whatever we can—our bodies through dancing or instruments through making music—in praise to God. The devotion focuses on how our praise unites with creation's praise. The meditation invites us to praise God with heart, mind, soul, and body: our whole being.

Devotion

Cross: Praise God, from whom all blessings flow,
Invitatory bead: praise God, all creatures here below.
Resurrection bead: Alleluia! Alleluia!
1st cruciform bead: God, you are praised above the heavens.

Week beads, set 1: With each bead recite, "Holy, holy, holy," the song the angels sing around God's throne.

2nd cruciform bead: God, creation sings your praise.

Week beads, set 2: Use each bead to focus on the wide variety of creation; trees, plants, animals.

3rd cruciform bead: God, through the skill you have given me, I can create instruments of praise.

Week beads, set 3: Use each bead to express gratitude for different musical instruments used in praising God.

4th cruciform bead: God, I will praise you with all that I have.

Week beads, set 4: With each bead recite, "With all that I am, I praise you."

Resurrection bead: Praise God, the source of all our gifts,

Invitatory bead: praise Jesus Christ whose power uplifts,

Cross: Praise the Spirit, Holy Spirit! Alleluia! Amen.

Meditation

With each bead: I praise you with heart, mind, soul and body; with all that I am, I praise you.

PRAISING THE TRINITY

The grace of the Lord Jesus Christ, the love of God,
and the fellowship of the Holy Spirit be with you all.

—2 CORINTHIANS 13:13

As Christians, we believe in a God who is three persons: God the Father, God the Son, and God the Holy Spirit. This is a holy mystery. What does it mean that we believe in the Trinity? The devotion is designed to help us relate to each person in the Trinity and to understand how this doctrine can shape our faith and ministry. The meditation serves to remind us of our ongoing fellowship with the triune God.

Devotion

Cross: In the name of the Father, Son, and Holy Spirit,
Invitatory bead: open my heart and mind
Resurrection Bead: to receive your grace.
1st cruciform bead: Father, you created me in your image and offer your unfathomable love.
Week beads, set 1: Use each bead to praise God the Father for creation and for deep, eternal love.
2nd cruciform bead: Lord Jesus, you came from heaven to heal me, comfort me, and teach me before offering your life for the forgiveness of my sins.

Week beads, set 2: Use each bead to praise God the Son for his ministry on earth and saving grace.

3rd cruciform bead: Holy Spirit, you are God's breath moving through me, guiding, inspiring, and calling me toward fellowship with creation and spiritual perfection.

Week beads, set 3: Use each bead to praise God the Holy Spirit for moving in your life.

4th cruciform bead: Holy Trinity, God in three persons, you perfectly exemplify love, trust, and holy relationship, calling me and the world toward perfect union.

Week beads, set 4: Use each bead to praise the Trinity and consider what you can learn from that perfect union.

Resurrection bead: In the name of the Father, Son, and Holy Spirit,

Invitatory bead: I receive your love, grace, and fellowship.

Cross: Amen.

Meditation

With each bead: Thanks be to God the Father, God the Son, and God the Holy Spirit.

PRAISING THE REIGN OF CHRIST

> Therefore, God highly honored him and gave him a name above all names, so that at the name of Jesus everyone in heaven, on earth, and under the earth might bow and every tongue confess that Jesus Christ is Lord, to the glory of God the Father.
>
> —PHILIPPIANS 2:9-11

In Philippians, Paul reminds us that confessing the name of Jesus is an act of praise and worship, one that unites our earthly worship with the worship of heaven and brings glory to God. The devotion invites us to confess the authority that has been given to the name of Jesus, while the meditation invites thought on the name Jesus.

Devotion

Cross: Lord Christ, as you once reigned over sin from the cross,

Invitatory bead: rule in my life now

Resurrection bead: that I might be raised to sing your eternal praise with all creation.

1ˢᵗ cruciform bead: Jesus, your name is exalted above all names.

Week beads, set 1: Use each bead to meditate on one of the titles associated with Jesus (Lord, Messiah,

Emmanuel, Christ, God's Son, the Human One, King of kings, etc.)

2nd cruciform bead: Lord, I bow before the mention of your name.

Week beads, set 2: Use each bead to confess Christ's power over anything or anyone trying to claim your loyalty.

3rd cruciform bead: Lord, your authority is proclaimed throughout creation.

Week beads, set 3: Use each bead to meditate on how confessing Christ brings you into fellowship with all who confess Christ.

4th cruciform bead: Lord, my confession of you brings glory to the full Godhead.

Week beads, set 4: Use each bead to meditate on the fellowship Jesus shares with the Father.

Resurrection bead: Glory be to you, Lord Christ,

Invitatory bead: and to the Father,

Cross: and to the Holy Spirit, now and forever. Amen.

Meditation

With each bead: Jesus, name above all names.

PRAISING THE GREAT I AM

Be still, and know that I am God!

—PSALM 46:10, NRSV

We spend so much of our lives being and doing, often at the expense of our physical, mental, and spiritual health. We act as if the fate of the world depends on us. Yet God reminds us many times that God is the great I AM. The fate of the world rests in God's hands, not ours. This is good news. We can simply be, resting in the knowledge of God's grace. The devotion offers us a chance to breathe and spend time knowing God. The meditation encourages us just to be still.

Devotion

Cross: In the name of the Father, Son, and Holy Spirit.
Invitatory bead: Amen.
Resurrection bead: *Take a deep, long breath.*
1st cruciform bead: Be still, and know that I am God!
Week beads, set 1: Use each bead to take a deep breath and know God.
2nd cruciform bead: Be still, and know that I am.
Week beads, set 2: Use each bead to take a deep breath and know I am.
3rd cruciform bead: Be still.

Week beads, set 3: Use each bead to take a deep breath and be still.

4th cruciform bead: Be.

Week beads, set 4: Use each bead to take a deep breath and just be.

Resurrection bead: God—the great I AM—lives

Invitatory bead: so that I can just be and rest in God's grace.

Cross: Amen.

Meditation

With each bead: Be still.

PRAISING FOREVER AND ALWAYS

Then I looked, and I heard the sound of many angels surrounding the throne, the living creatures, and the elders. They numbered in the millions—thousands upon thousands. They said in a loud voice, "Worthy is the slaughtered Lamb to receive power, wealth, wisdom, and might, and honor, glory, and blessing." And I heard every creature in heaven and on earth and under the earth and in the sea—I heard everything everywhere say, "Blessing, honor, glory, and power belong to the one seated on the throne and to the Lamb forever and always." Then the four living creatures said, "Amen," and the elders fell down and worshipped.

—REVELATION 5:11-14

The book of Revelation often seems confusing, even strange. John does his best to describe this God-given vision of the fulfillment of creation, but we humans struggle to understand the vision. However, the verses above carry power! Here, all of creation—all of it— comes together with the angels to praise God. The creatures and elders offer effusive praise with their whole being. The devotion invites us to place ourselves within this scene and join the unending praise of God. The meditation continues our praise of the Lamb.

36

Devotion

Cross: God of all creation,

Invitatory bead: out of your love you created us

Resurrection bead: so that we might spend eternity loving and glorifying you.

1st cruciform bead: We join with creation to surround your throne.

Week beads, set 1: Use each bead to envision yourself at the foot of God's throne with creation.

2nd cruciform bead: We sing your praises.

Week beads, set 2: Use each bead to offer loud praise to God.

3rd cruciform bead: We heard the shouts of "Amen."

Week beads, set 3: Use each bead to listen to the shouts of "Amen." So be it!

4th cruciform bead: With creation, we fall before you, worshiping you forever and always.

Week beads, set 4: Use each bead to envision yourself falling down and worshiping God.

Resurrection bead: Amen!

Invitatory bead: Amen!

Cross: Amen!

Meditation

With each bead: Worthy is the Lamb!

Prayers of
Confession

Who We Are in Relation to God

When we hear the word *confession*, we often think of being sorry in a religious context—sorrow over sin perhaps. However, we also use the word *confession* in terms of witnessing to our understanding of who God is—confessing our faith. Both of these ideas are important to the biblical sense of confession. They intertwine: Confessing our faith in who God is allows us to see ourselves differently; we see our failures and shortcomings and confess them as sins to God.

We have this dual sense of confession in mind when we describe confession as an understanding of who we are in relation to God. The scriptures we have chosen for the following devotions include both confessions of faith and confessions of sin. Use these prayers as ways to confess who you are in relation to God.

CONFESSING GOD'S GLORY

I said, "Mourn for me; I'm ruined! I'm a man with unclean lips, and I live among a people with unclean lips. Yet I've seen the king, the LORD of heavenly forces!"

Then one of the winged creatures flew to me, holding a glowing coal that he had taken from the altar with tongs. He touched my mouth and said, "See, this has touched your lips. Your guilt has departed, and your sin is removed."

—ISAIAH 6:5-7

Once Isaiah sees God for who God is, he sees himself in a new light. This new understanding before the glory of God moves Isaiah to confession of both God's majesty and his own sins. The devotion invites us to journey through Isaiah's confession. The meditation invites us to claim God's forgiveness.

Devotion

Cross: God, you are holy, holy, holy!

Invitatory bead: Cleanse my lips that my mouth may declare your praise.

Resurrection bead: Glory be to you, Father, Son and Holy Spirit; one God in perfect holiness.

1st cruciform bead: God, in your light I see my uncleanliness.

Week beads, set 1: Use each bead to confess whatever makes you feel unworthy to be in God's presence.

2nd cruciform bead: Purifying God, cleanse me as I confess your glory.

Week beads, set 2: Use each bead to accept God's forgiveness of whatever you confessed with set 1 of the week beads.

3rd cruciform bead: God, as you dwell in perfect community, so I dwell in a community of unclean people.

Week beads, set 3: Use each bead to confess communal sins.

4th cruciform bead: Lord, as you call us to live together in fellowship, heal us as a people.

Week beads, set 4: Use each bead to confess God's cleansing of our communal sins through Christ.

Resurrection bead: Cleanse us with the fire of your Spirit, O God,

Invitatory bead: that we may confess your glory through pure lives.

Cross: Pray the Lord's Prayer.

Meditation

With each bead: My sin is removed.

CONFESSING GOD'S FAITHFULNESS

> If we claim, "We don't have any sin," we deceive our-
> selves and the truth is not in us. But if we confess our
> sins, [God] is faithful and just to forgive us our sins and
> cleanse us from everything we've done wrong. If we
> claim, "We have never sinned," we make him a liar and
> his word is not in us.
>
> —1 JOHN 1:8-10

Sin is part of our lives. Thankfully, God's forgiveness is
equally universal. Confessing our sin allows us to experience the grace and cleansing God offers. The devotion
invites us to name our sins and claim God's forgiveness
of them. The meditation invites us to open our lives to
God's cleansing presence by meditating on the words
forgive and cleanse.

Devotion

Cross: Lord Christ, you reigned over sin by being lifted
    high on the cross.

Invitatory bead: Cleanse me from all my sins,

Resurrection bead: including the sin of thinking I am
    sinless.

1st cruciform bead: God of truth, help me not hide
    from the truth of my own sins.

42

Week beads, set 1: Use each bead to confess wrongs you have done.

2ⁿᵈ cruciform bead: Faithful God, your mercy is more abundant than my sins.

Week beads, set 2: Use each bead to speak God's mercy over any sins that came to mind in week beads, set 1.

3ʳᵈ cruciform bead: God of wisdom, you know me better than I know myself.

Week beads, set 3: Use each bead to ask God to shed light on sins that you may be prone to overlook within yourself.

4ᵗʰ cruciform bead: Cleansing God, wash and renew my heart.

Week beads, set 4: Use each bead to experience God's cleansing for the sins you confessed with week beads, set 3.

Resurrection bead: God of new birth,

Invitatory bead: may I be born anew by your forgiving presence in my life.

Cross: Pray the Lord's Prayer.

Meditation

With each bead: Forgive and cleanse me, O God.

CONFESSING GOD'S COMPASSION AND MERCY

> The LORD is compassionate and merciful, very patient,
> and full of faithful love. God won't always play the
> judge; he won't be angry forever. He doesn't deal with
> us according to our sin or repay us according to our
> wrongdoing, because as high as heaven is above the
> earth, that's how large God's faithful love is for those
> who honor him. As far as east is from west—that's how
> far God has removed our sin from us.
>
> —PSALM 103:8–12

When someone sins, we want judgment and retribu-
tion. However, we worship a compassionate God who
forgives our sins. Such worship can shape us, helping
us to view others with compassion and to practice forgiveness, even of our enemies. The devotion invites us
to consider God's mercy for us in the midst of our sin,
while the meditation encourages us to consider God's
compassionate nature.

Devotion

Cross: God of compassion and mercy,
Invitatory bead: in the midst of my sin
Resurrection bead: help me to see who you are.

44

1st cruciform bead: Even though I sin, you do not judge me.

Week beads, set 1: Use each week bead to recognize how God's treatment of sin can change the way you judge yourself and others.

2nd cruciform bead: Even though I sin, you are full of compassion for me.

Week beads, set 2: Use each week bead to experience God's compassion for you and to consider how you can share that compassion with others.

3rd cruciform bead: Even though I sin, you do not repay my sin with anger.

Week beads, set 3: Use each week bead to understand that God does not punish you or cast you aside when you sin.

4th cruciform bead: Even though I sin, you continue to love me deeply, faithfully.

Week beads, set 4: Use each bead to receive God's deep, faithful love for you.

Resurrection bead: In the name of Jesus Christ,

Invitatory bead: the living example of mercy.

Cross: Pray the Lord's Prayer.

Meditation

With each bead: The Lord is compassionate and merciful.

CONFESSING GOD'S FORGIVENESS

So I admitted my sin to you; I didn't conceal my guilt. "I'll confess my sins to the LORD," is what I said. Then you removed the guilt of my sin. *Selah* That's why all the faithful should pray to you during troubled times, so that a great flood of water won't reach them. You are my secret hideout! You protect me from trouble. You surround me with songs of rescue! *Selah*

—PSALM 32:5-7

Guilt tempts us to hide our sins. This deception becomes like a prison that holds us captive, lest we reveal our sin and be found out. Confession is not only naming our sin before God but also claiming God's power over our sin. Through confession God forgives our sin and rescues us from the power of guilt. We are freed to live in God's grace, not held in bondage by guilt. The devotion and meditation invite us to confess God's forgiveness and ponder God's power to redeem us.

Devotion

Cross: God of mercy,
Invitatory bead: let me hide in your grace,
Resurrection bead: that my sins and guilt may be removed from me.

1ˢᵗ cruciform bead: I confess that I sin by doing that which I should not do.

Week beads, set 1: Use each bead to confess to God sins of commission.

2ⁿᵈ cruciform bead: I confess that I sin by failing to do the good I can do.

Week beads, set 2: Use each bead to confess to God sins of omission.

3ʳᵈ cruciform bead: I confess that your power to forgive is stronger than my guilt.

Week beads, set 3: Use each bead to claim God's power over your sins of omission.

4ᵗʰ cruciform bead: I confess that your strength to remove my guilt is greater than my attempts to hide my faults.

Week beads, set 4: Use each bead to claim God's forgiveness of your sins of commission.

Resurrection bead: Raise me, O God, above the power of sin and guilt

Invitatory bead: that I may sing of your rescue.

Cross: Pray the Lord's Prayer.

Meditation

With each bead: You surround me with songs of rescue.

CONFESSING OUR SINS

Have mercy on me, God, according to your faithful love! Wipe away my wrongdoings according to your great compassion! Wash me completely clean of my guilt; purify me from my sin! Because I know my wrongdoings, my sin is always right in front of me.

—PSALM 51:1-3

Guilt makes it hard for us to forget our sins, but scripture tells us that God forgives and wipes away our sin. By naming our sins in confession, we claim God's power over them. The devotion invites us to name specific sins that may be troubling us so that we can move toward claiming God's forgiveness and power over these sins. The meditation asks us to consider how God desires to make us completely clean.

Devotion

Cross: Christ, on the hard wood of the cross you bore my sins.

Invitatory bead: Wash me now from the guilt of my sins

Resurrection bead: that I may live in your faithful love.

1st cruciform bead: Compassionate Lord, wipe away my wrongdoings.

Week beads, set 1: Use each bead to confess acts of wrong that you have done.

2nd cruciform bead: Merciful God, cleanse me.

Week beads, set 2: Use each bead to claim God's cleansing for the sins of commission you confessed with week beads, set 1.

3rd cruciform bead: Faithful Lord, your love remains steadfast, even when mine grows cold.

Week beads, set 3: Use each bead to confess things you have not done that you should have done.

4th cruciform bead: Holy God, purify me.

Week beads, set 4: Use each bead to claim God's forgiveness for these sins of omission confessed with week beads, set 3.

Resurrection bead: Lord of new life,

Invitatory bead: may I live in the light of your forgiveness.

Cross: Pray the Lord's Prayer.

Meditation

With each bead: Wash me completely clean.

CONFESSING OUR HOPE

> Let's hold on to the confession of our hope without wavering, because the one who made the promises is reliable.
>
> —HEBREWS 10:23

Hope is central to the Christian faith. Amidst the troubles and pain in the world, it is critical that we as Christians confess our hope. This type of confession can invite others to accept the joy and peace of the gospel in the midst of their suffering. The devotion focuses on confessing our hope personally and corporately as the church. The meditation invites listening for God's promises for our lives.

Devotion

Cross: ~~Pray the Lord's Prayer.~~

Invitatory bead: God of hope, as I long for the full coming of your kingdom,

Resurrection bead: strengthen me to live now in the hope of your promises spoken to us in Christ.

1st cruciform bead: Lord Christ, you have promised me the joys of eternal life.

Week beads, set 1: Use each bead to confess one of the promises Christ speaks to you.

2nd cruciform bead: Lord, help me to maintain hope amidst adversity.

Week beads, set 2: Confess worries, doubts, frustrations that may tempt you to lose hope.

3rd cruciform bead: God of hope, may your church celebrate your promises in the world.

Week beads, set 3: Use each bead to remember promises Christ has made to the people of God.

4th cruciform bead: God of promises, may we not lose heart as a people but cling to your promises.

Week beads, set 4: Confess what may be troubling your church at this time.

Resurrection bead: God, help me to stand on your promises

Invitatory bead: and confess my hope to the world.

Cross: Pray the Lord's Prayer.

Meditation

With each bead: God of hope, speak your promises to me.

CONFESSING CHRIST

"Everyone who acknowledges me before people, I also will acknowledge before my Father who is in heaven. But everyone who denies me before people, I also will deny before my Father who is in heaven."

—MATTHEW 10:32-33

Jesus promises to confess before the Father those who openly acknowledge him. Our public confession connects to the communion that God shares in God's own nature. The devotion invites us to meditate on opportunities to confess Jesus—opportunities accepted and missed. The meditation invites us to consider other areas of our lives where we can acknowledge Jesus the Christ.

Devotion

Cross: Lord, you publicly bore my sins on the cross.

Invitatory bead: Strengthen me to speak publicly of my allegiance to you

Resurrection bead: and not succumb to the temptation to deny you.

1st cruciform bead: O Lord, you are my Lord; I will acknowledge you.

Week beads, set 1: Use each bead to thank God for opportunities to tell others about Christ.

2nd cruciform bead: Lord, as you forgave Peter for his denial of you, forgive me for the times I have shied away from speaking aloud my loyalty to you.

Week beads, set 2: Use each bead to remember times you have failed to bear witness to Christ, and claim God's forgiveness for those moments.

3rd cruciform bead: God, you promise that through your Spirit you will give me the words I need to witness before others.

Week beads, set 3: Use each bead to thank God for the times when the Holy Spirit has guided you to speak words that others needed to hear.

4th cruciform bead: Son of God, I thank you that as I bear witness to you, you bear witness to me before the Father.

Week beads, set 4: Use each bead to celebrate Christ's invitation to communion with God.

Resurrection bead: Father, Son, and Holy Spirit,

Invitatory bead: make my life one with you.

Cross: Pray the Lord's Prayer.

Meditation

With each bead: With my life, I will acknowledge you.

PRAYERS OF
Intercession

Who We Are in Relation to God's Creation

Intercession may be the most familiar type of prayer for many of us. We often equate prayer with asking God for things. Intercession involves asking God on behalf of others, asking God to intervene in the circumstances of others or other situations within creation. This is also the place where we often address our personal needs before God.

The Bible exhorts Christians to pray not only for friends and for family but for all God's children, even our enemies. The following prayers of devotion and meditation focus on intercessions for a wide variety of people, including those we may pray for regularly and others for whom we have never known how to pray.

INTERCEDING FOR GOD'S CLEANSING

> I said, "Mourn for me; I'm ruined! I'm a man with
> unclean lips, and I live among a people with unclean
> lips. Yet I've seen the king, the LORD of heavenly forces!"
>
> —ISAIAH 6:5

Within Isaiah's confession of his own sin lies his
acknowledgment of the corporate sins of Israel: "I live
among a people with unclean lips." Later the prophet
will volunteer to take the message of God's holiness to
these people, offering them the same type of cleansing
that he experiences. This identification with the people
is part of the basis for intercession. The devotion invites
us to carry the corporate burdens—the burdens of the
"people" we are part of—before God. The meditation
bids us view ourselves as standing with these people.

Devotion

Cross: Triune God,

Invitatory bead: you dwell in perfect community.

Resurrection bead: Often our fellowship as humans is
distorted and sinful.

1st cruciform bead: I live among a people of unclean
lips.

Week beads, set 1: Use each bead to confess communal sins that impact your life.

2nd cruciform bead: Cleanse me with your holy fire.

Week beads, set 2: Use each bead to confess the power of God's ~~forgiveness~~. *to forgive the sinner*

3rd cruciform bead: O Lord of heavenly forces, your might is greater than all our sins.

Week beads, set 3: Use each bead to confess God's might.

4th cruciform bead: Enable me to carry your cleansing message to others..

Week beads, set 4: Use each bead to reflect on the words God may be giving you to speak to others.

Resurrection bead: ~~Father, Son~~ *Creator*, and Holy Spirit,

Invitatory bead: one God, forever and ever.

Cross: Pray the Lord's Prayer

Meditation

With each bead: I live among a people.

INTERCEDING FOR LOVE

> Jesus replied "The most important [commandment] is *Israel, listen! Our God is the one Lord, and you must love the Lord your God with all your heart, with all your being, with all your mind, and with all your strength.* The second is this, *You will love your neighbor as yourself.* No other commandment is greater than these."
>
> —MARK 12:29-31

With more than six hundred commandments in the Torah, the Jewish elders want Jesus to tell them which one is most important. They try to trap him. Jesus responds by reciting the Shema, the central commandment and prayer of the Jewish faith, which charges us to listen to and love God. He then tacks on a little-known commandment from Leviticus that implores us to love our neighbors as ourselves. The devotion encourages us to consider what it means to follow the greatest commandment, while the meditation reminds us to base our love on God's perfect love.

Devotion

Cross: God of love,
Invitatory bead: help me to listen
Resurrection bead: to your call to love.

1ˢᵗ cruciform bead: Lord God, help me to love you with my heart and soul.

Week beads, set 1: Use each bead to consider how you can love God with your heart and soul.

2ⁿᵈ cruciform bead: Lord God, help me to love you with my mind and strength.

Week beads, set 2: Use each bead to consider how you can love God with your mind and strength.

3ʳᵈ cruciform bead: Lord God, help me to love myself, given that I am created in your image and "was marvelously set apart" (Ps. 139:14).

Week beads, set 3: Use each bead to consider how you can love yourself and honor God's image within you.

4ᵗʰ cruciform bead: Lord God, help me love my neighbor.

Week beads, set 4: Use each bead to consider who your neighbors are and how you can love them and honor the image of God within them.

Resurrection bead: God of grace,

Invitatory bead: thank you for setting the example for perfect love.

Cross: Amen.

Meditation

With each bead: Help me to love as you love me.

INTERCEDING FOR STRENGTH

> Don't fear, because I am with you; don't be afraid, for I am your God. I will strengthen you, I will surely help you; I will hold you with my righteous strong hand.
>
> —ISAIAH 41:10

Fear can crop up at many points in our lives: transitions, difficult choices, loss of jobs or income or other forms of instability, new diagnoses, and death and grief. In times of fear we can feel alone, believing God is far away and has abandoned us. The Isaiah passage reminds us that God is with us in our fear, offering comfort, assistance, and courage. This provides an opportunity to explore the many reasons we have to "fear not." We can then take this assurance with us by using the meditation.

Devotion

Cross: Loving God,

Invitatory bead: you call me to you

Resurrection bead: through your Son, Jesus Christ.

1ˢᵗ cruciform bead: Lord, you are with me. I don't need to be afraid.

Week beads, set 1: Use each bead to feel God's presence, especially in the areas and places that scare you.

2nd cruciform bead: Lord, you are my God. I don't need to be afraid.

Week beads, set 2: Use each bead to feel God's mighty power, a power greater than anything you may fear.

3rd cruciform bead: Lord, you will strengthen and help me. I don't need to be afraid.

Week beads, set 3: Use each bead to recognize the ways in which God provides strength to you.

4th cruciform bead: Lord, you hold me with your strong hand. I don't need to be afraid.

Week beads, set 4: Use each bead to experience God's strong hand lifting you up, enabling you to move forward in confidence.

Resurrection bead: In the name of your son, Jesus, I pray.

Invitatory bead: Pray the Lord's Prayer.

Cross: Amen.

Meditation

With each bead: Lord, you are with me. I don't need to be afraid.

INTERCEDING FOR OUR OWN HEALING

> The living, the living can thank you, as I do today.
> Parents will tell children about your faithfulness. The
> LORD has truly saved me, and we will make music at
> the LORD's house all the days of our lives.
>
> —ISAIAH 38:19-20

King Hezekiah cries out to God in his deathly sickness.
God sends Isaiah to relay to the king that he will be
healed. The psalm of thanksgiving attributed to Hezekiah follows. Hezekiah's thanksgiving testifies to God's
faithfulness. The ability to pray for healing for ourselves—trusting that God will listen and respond—is
a great gift of our faith. The devotion offers a way to
pray for various types of healing, while the meditation
boldly calls upon the Lord for salvation.

Devotion

Cross: Merciful God, you hear my call when I cry out
to you;

Invitatory bead: you restore me through your healing
presence.

Resurrection bead: I thank you for restoring my life.

1st cruciform bead: I pray for healing in my body.

Week beads, set 1: Use each bead to pray for the health
of your body.

2nd cruciform bead: I pray for healing in my mind.

Week beads, set 2: Use each bead to pray for the health of your mind.

3rd cruciform bead: I pray for healing in my soul.

Week beads, set 3: Use each bead to pray for the health of your soul.

4th cruciform bead: I pray for healing in my heart.

Week beads, set 4: Use each bead to pray for the health of your heart.

Resurrection bead: God of salvation,

Invitatory bead: your presence restores my life

Cross: to proclaim your praise to future generations.

Meditation

With each bead: Lord, save me.

INTERCEDING FOR OTHERS' HEALING

I pray that the LORD answers you whenever you are in trouble. / Let the name of Jacob's God protect you. / Let God send help to you from the sanctuary / and support you from Zion. / Let God recall your many grain offerings; / let him savor your entirely burned offerings. *Selah* / Let God grant what is in your heart and fulfill all your plans. / Then we will rejoice that you've been helped. / We will fly our flags in the name of our God. / Let the LORD fulfill all your requests!

—PSALM 20:1-5

Even when we are not experiencing trouble in our personal lives, we know others who may be going through difficult circumstances. In the pain and agony of these troubles, they may feel unable to pray. By interceding for them we fulfill our commitment to support one another in the body of Christ. The devotion focuses on different types of trouble: mental, physical, relational, spiritual. The meditation invites us to consider God's protection amidst trouble.

Devotion

Cross: O Lord, you are our protector and helper;

Invitatory bead: I call upon you today for those who are in pain and trouble.

Resurrection bead: Support and strengthen them.

1st cruciform bead: God of grace, grant your help to those who are experiencing mental troubles.

Week beads, set 1: Use each bead to pray for someone who is suffering mental distress.

2nd cruciform bead: God of mercy, grant your healing to those who are experiencing physical ~~pain~~. *difficulties*

Week beads, set 2: Use each bead to intercede for someone who ~~is sick~~. *has physical challenges.*

3rd cruciform bead: God of compassion, grant your comfort to those who are experiencing relational difficulties.

Week beads, set 3: Use each bead to pray for someone who is troubled in a relationship.

4th cruciform bead: God of love, grant your strength to those who are experiencing spiritual troubles.

Week beads, set 4: Use each bead to intercede for someone who may be struggling with faith.

Resurrection bead: Faithful God, protect us all,

Invitatory bead: and help us in our times of trouble.

Cross: God, send your help and support to us. Amen.

Meditation

With each bead: "Let the name of Jacob's God protect you."

INTERCEDING FOR OUR LEADERS

> First of all, then, I ask that requests, prayers, petitions, and thanksgiving be made for all people. Pray for kings and everyone who is in authority so that we can live a quiet and peaceful life in complete godliness and dignity. This is right and it pleases God our savior, who wants all people to be saved and to come to a knowledge of the truth.
>
> —1 TIMOTHY 2:1-4

Complaining about, second-guessing, or challenging our leaders often seems easier than praying for them. First Timothy reminds us to pray for all people, especially those in positions of influence in our lives. The devotion invites us to pray for those who serve as leaders in our political, work, church, and personal lives. The meditation invites us to direct our lives to living in God's presence.

Devotion

Cross: O God, our savior,

Invitatory bead: we pray for our leaders

Resurrection bead: so that all people may live quiet and peaceful lives.

1st cruciform bead: I pray for leaders in my community and in the government.

Week beads, set 1: Use each bead to pray for different levels of government: local, national, international.

2nd cruciform bead: I pray for those who are in positions of influence in my work.

Week beads, set 2: Use each bead to pray for persons in positions of leadership in your place of work.

3rd cruciform bead: I pray for church leaders.

Week beads, set 3: Pray for those in positions of influence within your own congregation and throughout the church around the world.

4th cruciform bead: I pray for those who influence my personal life.

Week beads, set 4: Pray for individuals who mentor, inspire, and help you make decisions in your life.

Resurrection bead: O God, our savior,

Invitatory bead: may we all live in the light of your salvation

Cross: and the knowledge of your truth.

Meditation

With each bead: I pray that we may live peaceful lives with godliness and dignity.

INTERCEDING FOR CREATION

> The whole creation waits breathless with anticipation
> for the revelation of God's sons and daughters. Cre-
> ation was subjected to frustration . . . in the hope that
> the creation itself will be set free from slavery to decay
> and brought into the glorious freedom of God's chil-
> dren. We know that the whole creation is groaning
> together and suffering labor pains up until now.
>
> —ROMANS 8:19-22

God created everything and saw how good it was. And
God called us to care for creation. Yet war, poverty,
abuse, and other forms of violence; endangered spe-
cies; and enormous landfills indicate that we have not
always been faithful stewards. Just as we yearn for God
to redeem us, so also does creation yearn for redemp-
tion. This devotion helps us consider how we can be
better stewards, thereby participating in God's redemp-
tive act; the meditation reminds us that all are called to
this task.

Devotion

Cross: God of all,
Invitatory bead: hear the cries of your creation.
Resurrection bead: It calls out to you.
1st cruciform bead: You charged us with responsibility

for the earth, calling us to care for it.

Week beads, set 1: Use each bead to thank God for entrusting us with care for the world.

2nd cruciform bead: Yet we confess that we have not always been good stewards of creation and have contributed to its decay.

Week beads, set 2: Use each bead to consider the ways you have neglected to care for the earth.

3rd cruciform bead: We hear creation groaning as it suffers under our care.

Week beads, set 3: Use each bead to recognize the impact we have had on creation and the signs that the world is suffering.

4th cruciform bead: Help us to be good stewards of earth and its resources, leading it toward perfection through your redeeming love.

Week beads, set 4: Use each bead to pray for God's help in learning ways to better care for creation.

Resurrection bead: Be with us, O Lord,

Invitatory bead: as we await the perfection of creation.

Cross: Amen.

Meditation

With each bead: I am your faithful steward.

PRAYERS OF

Thanksgiving

Who God Is in Relation to Us

As we experience God in our lives, it moves us to respond in thanksgiving. The Greek word for thanksgiving, *eucharistia,* captures the dynamic of God's action toward us along with our reaction. Grace (*charis*) lies at the heart of thanksgiving. *The New Interpreter's Bible Dictionary* sums up this relationship in these words: "God grants grace; humans respond with thanksgiving. Perhaps thanksgiving may be best understood as the human response to the grace of God" (vol. 5, 547). The following prayers invite us to join in thanksgiving for the ways God graciously relates to us.

THANKSGIVING FOR GOD'S CALLING

Then I heard the Lord's voice saying, "Whom should I send, and who will go for us?"

I said, "I'm here; send me."

—ISAIAH 6:8

Part of our response to God's grace in our lives comes in offering ourselves for God's service. This is the type of thanks Isaiah offers for God's response to his confession and intercession, "I'm here; send me." Both the devotion and meditation that follow invite us to listen to where God may be calling us in service today.

Devotion

Cross: God, your mercy extends over all the earth,

Invitatory bead: and you call servants to go forth and proclaim your love.

Resurrection bead: You make me worthy to go forth in your service.

1st cruciform bead: Lord, when I hear your call, I shrink before my sense of unworthiness.

Week beads, set 1: Use each bead to name what hinders you from responding to God's call.

2nd cruciform bead: Lord, still you call my name.

Week beads, set 2: Use each bead to listen to God call your name.

3ʳᵈ cruciform bead: With your call comes the grace to respond.

Week beads, set 3: Use each bead to receive God's grace to respond.

4ᵗʰ cruciform bead: Through your cleansing presence, I respond and go.

Week beads, set 4: Use each bead to say, "I'm here; send me."

Resurrection bead: Missional God,

Invitatory bead: you have called me to your service, and you make me worthy of your love.

Cross: I go forth in thanksgiving.

Meditation

With each bead: "I'm here; send me."

THANKSGIVING FOR GOD'S DEEP LOVE

[The one who looked like a human being] said, "Don't be afraid. You are greatly treasured. All will be well with you. Be strong!"

—DANIEL 10:19

This passage summarizes our understanding of God as revealed in scripture: We do not need to be afraid. We can be at peace, trusting that God greatly treasures us and loves us deeply. As Julian of Norwich said, "All shall be well, and all shall be well, and all manner of thing shall be well." The devotion invites us to ponder and give thanks for this good news, while the meditation encourages us to rest in God's deep love for us.

Devotion

Cross: Loving God,

Invitatory bead: you call us out of our fear

Resurrection bead: to a place of peace.

1ˢᵗ cruciform bead: Thank you for transforming our fear into faith.

Week beads, set 1: Use each week bead to let God enter those places where you are fearful and where God can help you learn to trust.

2ⁿᵈ cruciform bead: Thank you for loving us deeply.

Week beads, set 2: Use each week bead to experience God's deep, rich, abundant, unconditional, steadfast, and all-encompassing love for you.

3rd cruciform bead: Help me be at peace, trusting that all shall be well.

Week beads, set 3: Use each week bead to practice trusting God, feeling the peace that comes from knowing that God loves you deeply.

4th cruciform bead: In thanksgiving, lead us to share this good news with others.

Week beads, set 4: Use each week bead to consider how you will share this good news of God's deep love and peace with others.

Resurrection bead: In the name of Jesus Christ, the Prince of Peace,

Invitatory bead: I pray.

Cross: Amen.

Meditation

With each bead: I am deeply loved by God.

THANKSGIVING FOR CREATION

> Everything that has been created by God is good, and nothing that is received with thanksgiving should be rejected.
>
> —1 TIMOTHY 4:4

Signs of God's power and majesty surround us. The mountains and oceans, the flowers and trees, the animals large and small—all reflect God's creativity and grace. Yet in the midst of our busy lives it is easy to take creation for granted. We take too little time to stop and enjoy the beautiful world that God created for our enjoyment. This devotion offers a moment to look around, see the beauty, and offer thanksgiving. The meditation helps us bask in thanksgiving for all God's gifts.

Devotion

Cross: God of the stars and the sky,

Invitatory bead: God of the ant and the elephant, the flowers and the rain,

Resurrection bead: you are everywhere and in all things.

1st cruciform bead: I thank you for all you have created.

Week beads, set 1: Use each bead to thank God for creation.

2nd cruciform bead: I see that everything is good.

Week beads, set 2: Use each bead to acknowledge the inherent goodness of creation.

3rd cruciform bead: I recognize your joy and love for me in all you created.

Week beads, set 3: Use each bead to recognize God's expression of love for you in creation.

4th cruciform bead: I receive this gift of love, and I honor it with love.

Week beads, set 4: Use each bead to consider how you can receive the gift of creation and honor it with your love.

Resurrection bead: Stars and moon, grass and lake,

Invitatory bead: you reveal God's majesty and love.

Cross: Thanks be to God.

Meditation

With each bead: Thank you for your gifts.

THANKSGIVING FOR EVERYONE

I thank my God every time I mention you in my prayers. I'm thankful for all of you every time I pray, and it's always a prayer full of joy. I'm glad because of the way you have been my partners in the ministry of the gospel from the time you first believed it until now. I'm sure about this: the one who started a good work in you will stay with you to complete the job by the day of Christ Jesus. . . . God is my witness that I feel affection for all of you with the compassion of Christ Jesus.

—PHILIPPIANS 1:3–8

It is easy to forget that Paul wrote this letter from prison. We do not normally associate the joy and thanksgiving Paul expresses in this short letter with someone in his circumstances. We gladly offer thanks when good things happen to us, but what about in times of difficulty? Look at what Paul gives thanks for even in prison. Does his list help us identify what to give thanks for in our current circumstances?

Devotion

Cross: I thank you, God, for the gift of prayer.
Invitatory bead: Increase my joy in prayer,
Resurrection bead: through your son, Jesus Christ.

1ˢᵗ cruciform bead: I am glad for those who share this life with me.

Week beads, set 1: Use each bead to give thanks for people you feel connected to in Christ.

2ⁿᵈ cruciform bead: I feel confident that you will continue and complete your work.

Week beads, set 2: Use each bead to pray for ministries where God is working to transform lives.

3ʳᵈ cruciform bead: I thank you for my friends in good and bad times.

Week beads, set 3: Use each bead to pray for those who have provided support in your life.

4ᵗʰ cruciform bead: I thank you for the way your compassion opens me to new relationships.

Week beads, set 4: Use each bead to pray for Christians throughout the world.

Resurrection bead: Christ, may your compassion grow within me as I grow in you.

Invitatory bead: Pray the Lord's Prayer.

Cross: In the name of the Father, Son, and Holy Spirit. Amen.

Meditation

With each bead: I thank my God for all of you.

THANKSGIVING FOR GOD'S BLESSING

The LORD bless you and keep you. The LORD make his face shine on you and be gracious to you. The LORD lift up his face to you and grant you peace.

—NUMBERS 6:24-26

God instructs Moses to offer this blessing to the Israelites at a time when they are struggling. They have been wandering in the desert for many years. They are tired, frustrated, and feeling abandoned by God. We too experience joy and hardship in our lives. At times we feel fatigued, frustrated, grieved, and angry. Sometimes we may feel abandoned by God. In those times we can remember this blessing. We can remember that God is with us and that God's face always shines on us. We can remember that God offers us all-encompassing peace to lead us through the hardships and the joys of our lives. And we can give thanks.

Devotion

Cross: God of abundant love,
Invitatory bead: you express your love in many ways
Resurrection bead: through your son, Jesus Christ.
1ˢᵗ **cruciform bead:** Thank you for blessing me and
protecting me.

Week beads, set 1: Use each bead to feel God's blessing and protection.

2nd cruciform bead: Thank you for shining your face on me.

Week beads, set 2: Use each bead to feel the warmth and love of God's face shining on you.

3rd cruciform bead: Thank you for being so gracious to me.

Week beads, set 3: Use each bead to consider the many ways in which the Lord is gracious to you, and give thanks.

4th cruciform bead: Thank you for your gift of peace.

Week beads, set 4: Use each bead to receive God's gift of peace, to give thanks for it, and to consider the ways in which you can live into God's peace.

Resurrection bead: In the name of Jesus Christ,

Invitatory bead: who perfectly embodied your peace.

Cross: Amen.

Meditation

With each bead: I live in God's peace.

THANKSGIVING FOR THE GOSPEL

Finally, brothers and sisters, pray for [Paul, Silvanus, and Timothy] so that the Lord's message will spread quickly and be honored, just like it happened with you. Pray too that we will be rescued from inappropriate and evil people since everyone that we meet won't respond with faith.

—2 THESSALONIANS 3:1–2

Paul asks the Thessalonians to share in his missionary and evangelistic work through prayer. Even if we feel ill-equipped to share the gospel with others, we all can pray for the spread of the gospel. The devotion focuses on praying for those who regularly share the gospel with others, as well as the opportunities we may receive to share this message with others. The meditation considers the spread of the gospel.

Devotion

Cross: Lord, you have commissioned us to carry your gospel to the ends of the earth.

Invitatory bead: Today I pray for Christians around the world who are sharing the message of your love

Resurrection bead: that others may come into the joy of fellowship with you.

1st cruciform bead: I pray for missionaries who bring your message to those who have never heard it before.

Week beads, set 1: Use each bead to pray for the spread of the gospel in various places.

2nd cruciform bead: I pray for pastors and teachers who present your gospel to Christians week after week.

Week beads, set 2: Use each bead to pray for pastors and Christian educators you know.

3rd cruciform bead: I pray that others may hear your hope and peace through my speaking today.

Week beads, set 3: Use each bead to pray for those you will encounter today.

4th cruciform bead: I pray that others will respond to the gospel in faith.

Week beads, set 4: Pray for those who may hear the gospel message.

Resurrection bead: Lord, I give thanks that your gospel continues to bring new life.

Invitatory bead: May the grace of your Spirit give me the words to articulate this life-giving message

Cross: and be united in one family of faith. Amen.

Meditation

With each bead: Lord, may your gospel spread quickly.

THANKSGIVING FOR ETERNAL LIFE

> Jesus said to [Martha], "I am the resurrection and the life. Whoever believes in me will live, even though they die. Everyone who lives and believes in me will never die. Do you believe this?" She replied, "Yes, Lord, I believe that you are the Christ, God's Son, the one who is coming into the world."
>
> —JOHN 11:25-27

Everything leads to this: God desires to be in relationship with us for all eternity. But our sin disconnects us from God. Jesus, by his life, death, and resurrection, reaches across that chasm and reclaims us. We need only to believe in him and proclaim that he is the Christ to receive the gift he offers: eternal life. With this devotion we can do just that, thanking Jesus for his gift of grace. The meditation affirms our belief in Jesus the Messiah.

Devotion

Cross: Jesus Christ,

Invitatory bead: you died so that I may live

Resurrection bead: with you in glory.

1st cruciform bead: You are the resurrection and the life.

Week beads, set 1: Use each bead to thank Jesus for being the resurrection and the life.

2nd cruciform bead: You offer me life, even though I may die.

Week beads, set 2: Use each bead to thank Jesus for the offer of life after death.

3rd cruciform bead: I believe that you are the Christ, God's son.

Week beads, set 3: Use each bead to proclaim your belief in Jesus the Christ.

4th cruciform bead: Thank you for your gift of eternal life.

Week beads, set 4: Use each bead to offer generous thanksgiving for Christ's gift of eternal life.

Resurrection bead: Jesus is the Christ,

Invitatory bead: the eternal King.

Cross: Thanks be to God.

Meditation

With each bead: I believe you are the Christ.

LEADER'S GUIDE

This book lends itself to a variety of uses with groups. We offer several ideas for weekly group gatherings as well as for use in other settings and in family devotions Choose the format and time frame that best fits your needs and interests or create your own.

For Weekly Study

The most obvious way to arrange your sessions is to focus your meetings on each section of the book in sequence (praise, confession, intercession, and thanksgiving). You could meet once to introduce the study (and possibly make prayer beads). You would then devote the next four weeks to one section each week, unless you choose to take your time and spend two to three weeks on each of the different prayer types. A longer period on each type permits an opportunity to explore these forms of prayer in a deeper way.

Another approach for a series is to pray one devotion from each of the four sections every week, experiencing all the types of prayer. With seven devotions per section, this would result in seven weeks of study with an additional week for the introduction. Alternatively, you could pray two devotions per week to make a fifteen-week (including the introduction) study.

MEETING AND ROOM SETUP

One hour is sufficient time for weekly meetings. As the leader, plan to arrive fifteen minutes early to prepare the room.

We recommend arranging chairs around a table so that group members face one another. This arrangement will facilitate dialogue as well as allow space for books, prayer beads, and notes. If a table is not available, arrange chairs in a circle.

Think about ways to create a prayerful mood in the room where the group gathers. Perhaps you can light a candle and play soft instrumental music in the background as members arrive or set up a small worship center with a cross and Bible. There is no need to make this complicated; simple settings often lend themselves to a spirit of prayer.

PRAYER BEADS

While it is possible for people to participate in this study without prayer beads, we encourage group members to obtain a set. Having prayer beads will make the study more meaningful. Participants can choose to borrow, purchase, or make prayer beads. Making prayer beads together with the group offers a meaningful bonding experience, particularly for groups in which members may not know one another well. If you choose to make prayer beads with your group, we advise you to add an additional week to your study and use the initial meeting for prayer bead making. Instructions for making prayer beads follow this Leader's Guide.

INTRODUCTORY MEETING

Since this will be the first time for these people to meet (unless they met previously to make prayer beads), take time to welcome each participant. Offer an opening prayer such as the following:

> Loving God we praise you for the many ways you make yourself known to us. In this time together may we be open to your presence in and among us. Be in our thoughts and in our speaking as we share with one another the ways we connect with you. Amen.

Then invite each person to introduce himself or herself. As part of the introductions, suggest that they

- Tell aloud what drew them to this series on praying with beads. How did they hear about the study? What about the study interested them? Have they prayed with beads before?

- Raise questions related to what they hope to receive from this study. What do they want to learn?

- Show their prayer beads to the group. Encourage them to talk about the beads: Did they make the set? If so, how did they choose the colors or design? What was meaningful about the process of making the set? If they did not make the prayer beads, where did they get them? Why did they choose that particular set? Was it given to them as a gift?

Next, orient the group members to the study. Review the study outline: The study takes place over five to fifteen weeks (depending upon your choices about the series), with one to three weeks devoted to each of the four sections. Each section includes a brief introduction followed by seven prayers. The prayers begin with a scripture passage and an introduction. This is followed by a devotion that offers specific prompts for each of the prayer bead sections and a meditation— a brief phrase designed for use on every bead.

Encourage the participants to do the following:

- Spend five minutes on the first day of the week

reading the introduction to the section.

- Spend five to ten minutes reading the scripture passage and introduction for the particular prayer.
- Spend at least five minutes each day praying either the devotion or meditation (or both) with their prayer beads.

This will guarantee that each person benefits as much as possible from the study.

Assure the participants that they do not have to view the devotion as a script; they do not need to try to hold the book in one hand and read word-for-word while using their other hand to finger the prayer beads. It may be helpful for them to read through the devotion one time to get a sense of what it is about, then lay the book down and pray with their prayer beads.

Group members also need to understand that some of the devotions may be more comfortable or compelling than others, and that is okay. We have provided a variety of devotions to show the many ways prayer beads can be used to praise, confess, intercede, and give thanks. Members will find that they prefer some prayers over others, just as they may prefer the devotions over the meditations (or vice versa). Still, we encourage participants to try each prayer and to use both the devotion and meditation at least once. Doing so may introduce them to new ways of connecting with God as well as help them consider what types of prayer work best for them.

In closing, ask the group members to hold their prayer beads in their hands. Explain that you will bless the beads using the following prayer:

Gracious God,

We praise you for your abundant love as you seek to connect with us through prayer.

We thank you for the many ways in which we can connect with you, including through the use of prayer beads.

We ask your blessing upon these beads. May they remind us of your loving presence. May we use them to help us praise you, confess to you, lift up intercessions to you, and offer our thanks to you. May they also help us to be still and listen to what you have to say to us.

We pray this in Jesus' name. Amen.

WEEKLY FORMAT

OPENING

When all participants arrive and find a seat, take a moment to help everyone transition from the noise and rush of daily life to this time of reflection and discussion. Encourage participants to hold their prayer beads, close their eyes, and take three deep breaths. This does not have to be formal; let it be an opportunity to relax and be still in God's presence.

PRAY A DEVOTION TOGETHER

Each week identify one person to be the leader. The leader will choose one of the devotions from that week to read while participants hold their prayer beads and follow along with each bead. When the leader comes to the cruciform bead, he or she will read the line from the devotion for that particular bead aloud, then allow time for silence as the participants pray silently while fingering each of the seven week beads. After providing a sufficient amount of time for the participants to pray with all seven week beads (about one minute), the leader will read the prayer for the next cruciform bead. Continue in this way through the conclusion of the prayer.

SET THE CONTEXT

As the leader, look ahead to the upcoming week to familiarize yourself with the content. Then use the following suggested script to help prepare the group for each week's lesson.

PRAISE: We are a part of God's creation. Praise acknowledges our relationship with God amidst all of creation. Awe, wonder, and gratitude for God's actions in our life and the world are ways to express praise. The devotions and meditations in the praise section will help participants explore various times and places that have evoked their praise. Encourage them to think about other scripture passages or times that may move them to praise.

CONFESSION: Acknowledging who we are in relationship to God is at the heart of confession. Confession can include naming our sins, what separates us from God. Confession is also a statement of faith: who we believe God is. Do participants tend to think about one of these aspects of confession to the exclusion of the other? The devotions and meditations in the confession section play off both ideas of confession. See if they help you understand the relationship between confessing faith and confessing sin.

INTERCESSION: Understanding how we relate to one another before God is part of what moves us to intercede for others. Prayer for others may seem more common or familiar to us in our personal prayers. See if any of the devotions or meditations for this week move

participants to pray for people they do not often intercede for. Can they think of ways to incorporate these
people into their regular prayers?

THANKSGIVING: God relates to us personally.
Thanksgiving is about recognizing God's presence in
our midst. The prayers and meditations in the Thanksgiving section illustrate how we can thank God for
divine activity in our personal lives and our communal life. What other times or circumstances might evoke
thanksgiving?

Review the Week's Prayers

Use any or all of the following questions to facilitate
discussion about the week's section. You may choose
to take each question in order. Read it aloud and
give group members time to respond. Another option
would entail inviting group members to speak about
the questions they found most thought-provoking.

You may not have the answers to all the questions. That is okay. Do the best you can and feel free to
invite responses from others in the group. If you have
the opportunity, consider reviewing other resources on
praise, confession, intercession, thanksgiving. If you do
not know the answer to a question, invite group members to do additional research.

- What did you learn about praise (or confession, intercession, thanksgiving) from this section?

- How do you normally offer praise (or confession, intercession, thanksgiving) to God?

- What makes it easy or difficult for you to offer praise (or confession, intercession, thanksgiving) to God?

- How do you feel when you pray in this way? What are your thoughts?

- What was your favorite prayer for this week's section? Why?

- What was your least favorite devotion for this week's section? Why?

- How did using prayer beads to offer praise (or confession, intercession, thanksgiving) impact your prayer? Did it enhance it? Why or why not?

Create an environment in which every participant feels encouraged to share without putting undue pressure on those who prefer to remain silent. If you find yourself leading an unusually quiet group, experiment with ways of motivating each member to participate.

SHARE OBSERVATIONS

The questions below may start conversation or foster the sharing of participants' thoughts about the prayers.

- How did the devotion and meditation help in your understanding of the use of prayer beads?
- How did the devotion and meditation help in your understanding of different ways of praying?
- How did the devotion and meditation aid your understanding of connecting and communicating with God?

CLOSING

Invite a participant to lead the group through one of the meditations from this week. The leader will invite the group members to pray, then read aloud the phrase to be prayed. The leader will then allow time for group members to pray the words silently as they finger the beads (about one minute). The leader will then close the prayer with "Amen."

To Open Meetings

The prayers in this book may be used as devotions for meetings. Many churches have prayer teams that meet on a regular basis—often weekly—to pray for the needs of the congregation and community. In addition, other groups meet regularly and desire a time of devotion to begin their time together. Persons can choose the devotion that best represents the particular needs of the group at the time.

In such situations, not every group member will have a set of prayer beads. Do not allow this to deter the use of these devotions. Although they are written for use with prayer beads, people can pray them without beads. The leader can read the devotion prompts aloud until he or she reaches the prompt for the week beads. At that time, the leader can pause for a time of silence while the group members pray silently, either with or without prayer beads. The leader can also make sets of prayer beads available for use by group members; these sets can be made by volunteers and kept on hand for such times.

Praying in this way can provide an opportunity to introduce new people to the use of beads in prayer.

For Use in Family Devotions

Prayer beads offer a wonderful tool for use in family devotions. The shiny, colorful beads can draw children into prayer and get them excited about praying. They can also help them feel connected to God and give them some structure for their prayer time.

Children really enjoy making prayer beads. They like to think about how they will use the beads to talk with God and choosing bead colors that have meaning for them. Using the instructions included in this book, a child of any age could make a set of prayer beads with some assistance. Often when we work with children we have them make a chaplet—a set of prayer beads with two sets of seven beads rather than four. This smaller size fits well in their hands and may be more appropriate for their attention span.

You may also choose to use other materials for prayer beads, particularly for very young children, such as chenille stems and pony beads; macaroni or cereal that will work well on string; paracord or twine that can be tied into knots; pop beads; or large wooden beads or blocks with laces. Get creative! And don't get hung up on whether the set of beads has an invitatory bead, a cruciform bead, etc. Encourage the child to design his or her own set of prayer beads, then accommodate the prayers to fit. You will notice in the prayers that follow that while the intent is the same, the format differs to invite children to participate.

VARIOUS TYPES OF CHILDREN'S PRAYER BEADS

The devotions and meditations in this book may provide an opportunity for families to talk about different ways of praying to God. To help with this, we offer one sample prayer from each of the four prayer types below. These will introduce children to the idea of praising, confessing, interceding, and offering thanks to God. As children become comfortable with these forms of prayers, families may use some of the prayers in this book to continue to build their confidence level and encourage new ways to express themselves to God.

When using these prayers with children, it is particularly important that they understand these prayers are not scripts. They do not have to read the prayers word for word. Review the prayer together as a family, then encourage each member to pray from the heart. Children need to know there is no wrong way to pray, and no wrong way to use prayer beads.

PRAISE

Praise is a way of letting someone know you like them or admire them. Can you think of people you like a lot? What would you say about them? When we praise God, we take time to tell God how much we like God. We can say things like, "You are great, God!" "I really love you!" or "God, you make a great rainbow!" Try praising God with this prayer:

First bead or cross: Dear God,
Second bead: I think that you are
With each bead: [Say something in praise of God.]
Last bead or cross: Amen.

CONFESSION

Have you ever done something you weren't proud of, or that you shouldn't have done? How did it make you feel? Did you tell someone what you did? Was that hard? Confession is a big word that describes how we tell God about the things we should not have done. It is also our time to remember that God loves us and forgives us, even when we don't always do what we are supposed to, so it is safe to confess to God.

First bead or cross: Dear God,
Second bead: I need to tell you that:
With each bead: [Tell God about any situation that you feel sad or worried about.]
Last bead or cross: Amen.

INTERCESSION

Do you know anyone who needs help? Do you have a friend or family member who is sick or sad? Or is there something you need help with from God? Intercession is our way of telling God about the people who need God's help. Have you ever prayed, "God bless Dad. God bless Grandma"? That is a way of asking God to take care of that person. Even though God already knows what we need, sometime it helps us if we can tell God what we need or ask God to help other people. Use this prayer to share with God:

First bead or cross: Dear God,
Second bead: please help (or bless)
With each bead: [Name yourself and other people who need God's help or blessing.]
Last bead or cross: Amen.

THANKSGIVING

What are you thankful for? What makes you happy? Thanksgiving gives us a time to say "thanks" to God. God loves us deeply and is always working in our lives. What are some things you can thank God for?

First bead or cross: Dear God,
Second bead: thank you for
With each bead: [Tell God what you are thankful for.]
Last bead or cross: Amen.

MAKING PRAYER BEADS

If you plan to make prayer beads with your group, we recommend you set aside about one hour. If you plan to discuss the information in the Introduction as well, set aside one and one-half to two hours. This session would be prior to the first study session.

To maximize your time, review the following instructions. Prior to the bead-making session, consider watching the instructional video found at

http://abeadnaprayer.wordpress.com/2013/05/02/video-how-to-make-prayer-beads/

Even better, by making a set of prayer beads in advance you ensure your own preparation to lead group members through this activity and have a sample set to show them. You will serve as their inspiration!

APPROACHES AND SKILL LEVELS

- If you have plenty of time for the bead-making session, I recommend purchasing beads in a variety of colors and allowing the participants to create their own designs. This approach can encourage people to give thought to the color and composition of this prayer tool.

- If you have limited time, I suggest you prepare "kits" in advance. Each kit would contain all the materials one person would need to complete a set of prayer beads, except for the tools and crimp tubes. You might offer some variety among the kits—such as two or three different color combinations—to allow for some choice and individualization.

You will also want to consider the participants' *skill level* when it comes to working with beads.

- If you have one or two *experienced participants* who have worked with beads and the rest have *little or no background*, I recommend that you attach the crosses to the wire ahead of time (see Step 1, page 110). This saves time and frustration and makes the prayer bead-making session much more enjoyable.
- If you are working with a group of *skilled beaders,* they may feel quite capable of attaching the cross to the wire themselves.

In addition to the beads, I recommend having a small bowl or tray for each participant to collect his or her beads or to hold the kit as the prayer beads are assembled.

THE CRIMP TUBES

Successful completion of prayer beads is due, in large part, to the crimp tubes. Although tiny, these tubes serve a critical function in the formation of the prayer beads. Allow me to stress three aspects:

1. Distribute the crimp tubes separately from the other prayer bead materials. The reason for this is simple: The tiny crimp tubes can easily get lost if mixed with a larger bag or bowl of beads. Whether I use preassembled kits or allow participants to choose their own beads, I always pass out the crimp tubes myself, carefully placing them in front of the participants and drawing their attention to them. It might help to assign a crimp-tube distributor.

2. Make sure participants understand the placement of the crimp tubes on their wires. They must add the crimp tubes to the wire early on in the process rather than adding them later. If someone strings all the beads on the wire and realizes he or she has forgotten to add the crimp tube, that person will have to undo the set and start all over.

3. Be prepared to provide assistance to participants who need help threading the crimp tubes onto the wire. Again, you might consider having someone who distributes and provides assistance with the crimp tubes.

THE TOOLS

A crucial piece to making prayer beads is the tools. The good news is that beading requires only two tools: chain nose pliers and side wire cutters. The even better news is that you can find both of these tools at a craft store, a hardware store, or in your family's toolbox. If you have no beading experience, I would encourage you to practice using the tools before leading the group through this activity.

I recommend that you identify one person to be in charge of "tying off" the prayer beads (if you have more than one person who can do this, all the better). This person sits at a table with the tools. As participants finish stringing their beads together, they can bring their sets to the tool person. The tool person can then complete Steps 13–14.

ROOM SETUP

Making prayer beads can be a good group-building activity. People seem to enjoy talking and bonding with one another as they string their beads. I recommend using round or rectangular tables where people can sit facing one another. If that is not possible, a classroom or training room setup will work as well.

At the front, side, or back of the room, set up a

table where you can lay out all of the bead-making supplies or kits. This may be the same table where the identified tool person sits to tie off the prayer beads.

Consider adding other enhancements to this experience such as:

- a music player available to play Taizé or other soft background music;
- completed sets of prayer beads around the room for people to see;
- snacks or beverages.

Making a set of prayer beads is fairly easy, even if you have no prior beading experience. I have provided instructions below. These instructions are illustrated in a video at http://abeadnaprayer.wordpress.com/2013/05/02/video-how-to-make-prayer-beads/.

The materials listed below can be purchased at a local craft store. My company, Prayerworks Studio, also offers kits, which include the necessary materials (but not the tools). You may purchase the kits at www.prayerworksstudio.etsy.com. Use the discount code BOOK20 to receive 20% off your purchase.

MATERIALS NEEDED

5 large (10mm–12mm) beads
29 medium (8mm–10mm) beads
36 seed (size #6 or #8) beads
1 cross or other pendant
2 crimp tubes (size 2 x 2)
20–24 inches of wire (49 strand, .18 or .19 inches)

TOOLS REQUIRED

1 pair of chain nose pliers
1 set of side wire cutters

INSTRUCTIONS

L = Large bead (cruciform and invitatory)

M = Medium bead (week and resurrection)

s = seed bead

STEP 1: Thread one of the crimp tubes onto the wire, then add the cross. (See figure 1.) Thread the end of the wire back up through the crimp tube. This will leave you with the two ends of the wire coming out of the crimp tube: the primary length of wire and a smaller "tail," about one inch in length. Using the pliers, squeeze the crimp tube until it is flattened. (See figure 2.)

FIGURE 1

FIGURE 2

STEP 2: String the beads in the following pattern, taking them all the way down so that the first bead aligns with the crimp tube that sits above the cross. (Note: make sure the beads cover both wires—the primary wire and the extra piece that extends from the top of the cross):

s L s M s L s

STEP 3: String the crimp tube (*this is a critical step!*).

STEP 4: String the first section of week beads in the following pattern: s M (7 times), then 1 s. It will look like this:

s M s M s M s M s M s M s M s

STEP 5: String 1 L bead.

STEP 6: String the second section of week beads by repeating Step 4.

STEP 7: String 1 L bead.

STEP 8: String the third section of week beads by repeating Step 4.

STEP 9: String 1 L bead.

STEP 10: String the fourth section of week beads by repeating Step 4.

STEP 11: Take the end of the wire and thread it back through the crimp tube that was added in STEP 3 (the wire will be heading back toward the cross; see figure 3). Thread it through the crimp tube, the seed bead, the large bead, the seed bead, and the medium bead so that it comes out from the bottom of the medium bead.

FIGURE 3

STEP 12: Pull the wire tightly, adjusting the beads as necessary to remove any slack in the wire and to ensure that the wire is completely covered up by the beads (figure 4). This is a good time to count all the beads and double check your pattern to be sure the beads are in the order you desire. If not, make the necessary changes before proceeding to the next step.

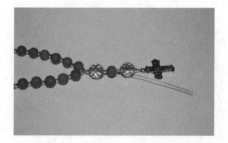

STEP 13: Using a pair of chain nose pliers, flatten the crimp tube as tightly as possible.

STEP 14: Using a set of side wire cutters, cut the remaining wire off as close to the beads as possible.

COMPLETED SET
Enjoy your beads! Blessings!

All prayer bead instruction photos are courtesy of
Blanka Gresham

WRITE YOUR OWN PRAYER

Just as prayer beads are a tool, these devotions and meditations are tools to help grow your own practice of prayer. Now try writing your own devotion and meditation. Perhaps you can begin with a passage of scripture that speaks to your life. How can it be worked into a devotion? Is there one phrase that you want to meditate on?

The template on the next page will help you organize your prayer.

Devotion

Cross:

Invitatory bead:

Resurrection bead:

1st cruciform bead:

Week beads, set 1:

2nd cruciform bead:

Week beads, set 2:

3rd cruciform bead:

Week beads, set 3:

4th cruciform bead:

Week beads, set 4:

Resurrection bead:

Invitatory bead:

Cross:

Meditation

With each bead:

RESOURCES

THE FOLLOWING WEBSITES will satisfy your interest in purchasing prayer beads or the materials to make your own prayer beads and in learning more about this prayer tool.

PRAYER BEADS

www.prayerworksstudio.etsy.com (use discount code BOOK20 to receive 20% off your purchase)
www.etsy.com/shop/prayerbedes
www.fullcirclebeads.com
www.solitariesofdekoven.org/store.html

BEADS AND MATERIALS

www.firemountaingems.com
www.goodybeads.com

MORE INFORMATION

www.abeadnaprayer.wordpress.com
www.kingofpeace.org/prayerbeads.htm
www.kimberlywinston.wordpress.com
www.prayerbedes.com

To read more about Protestant or other types of prayer beads, consider the following:

BOOKS ON PRAYER BEADS

Bauman, Lynn C. *The Anglican Rosary.* Telephone, TX: Praxis, 2003.

Brown, Patricia D. *Paths to Prayer: Finding Your Own Way to the Presence of God.* San Francisco: Jossey-Bass. 2003.

Doerr, Nan Lewis, and Virginia Stem Owens. *Praying with Beads: Daily Prayers for the Christian Year.* Grand Rapids, MI: William B. Eerdmans Publishing Company, 2007.

Ellsworth, Wendy. *Beading—the Creative Spirit: Finding Your Sacred Center through the Art of Beadwork.* Woodstock, VT: SkyLight Paths Publishing, 2009.

Kasten, Patricia Ann. *Linking Your Beads: The Rosary's History, Mysteries, and Prayers.* Huntington, IN: Our Sunday Visitor Publishing Division, 2011.

Ward, J. Neville. *Five for Sorrow, Ten for Joy: A Consideration of the Rosary.* Cambridge, MA: Cowley Publications, 1985.

Wiley, Eleanor, and Maggie Oman Shannon. *A String and a Prayer: How to Make and Use Prayer Beads.* Newburyport, MA: Red Wheel/Weiser, 2002.

Winston, Kimberly. *Bead One, Pray Too: A Guide to Making and Using Prayer Beads.* Harrisburg, PA: Morehouse Publishing, 2008.

BOOKS ON PRAYER AND SPIRITUAL DISCIPLINES

Benson, Robert. *Living Prayer*. New York: Jeremy P. Tarcher/Penguin, 1998.

Bloesch, Donald G. *The Struggle of Prayer*. New York: Harper & Row, 1980.

Bondi, Roberta C. *To Pray and to Love: Conversations on Prayer with the Early Church*. Minneapolis, MN: Augsburg Fortress, 1991.

Canham, Elizabeth J. *Finding Your Voice in the Psalms: An Invitation to Honest Prayer*. Nashville, TN: Upper Room Books, 2013.

————. *Heart Whispers: Benedictine Wisdom for Today*. Nashville, TN: Upper Room Books, 1999.

Foster, Richard. *Prayer: Finding the Heart's True Home*. New York: HarperCollins Publishers, 1992.

Harper, Steve. *A Pocket Guide to Prayer*. Nashville, TN: Upper Room Books, 2010.

Lamott, Anne. *Help, Thanks, Wow: The Three Essential Prayers*. New York: Penguin Group, 2012.

Merton, Thomas. *New Seeds of Contemplation*. New York: New Directions Paperback, 1961.

Tickle, Phyllis. *The Divine Hours: Pocket Edition*. New York: Oxford University Press, 2007.

Ulanov, Ann and Barry. *Primary Speech: A Psychology of Prayer*. Louisville, KY: Westminster John Knox, 1983.

von Balthasar, Hans Urs. *Prayer*. San Francisco: Ignatius Press, 1986.

Gerald Patrick Photography

MEET THE AUTHORS

KRISTEN E. VINCENT is the award-winning author of *A Bead and a Prayer: A Beginner's Guide to Protestant Prayer Beads,* published by Upper Room Books. She travels extensively to speak and lead retreats on prayer and prayer beads. She is also the owner and principal artisan of Prayerworks Studio, where she creates handcrafted prayer tools. She loves dark chocolate, gadgets, and the mountains. She remains committed to her lifelong quest for the perfect chocolate mousse.

MAX O. VINCENT is a United Methodist minister. He has served as a hospital chaplain and pastor of churches in North Carolina and Georgia. Currently, he is the pastor of Allen Memorial United Methodist Church in Oxford, Georgia. He is an adjunct faculty member at Oxford College of Emory University. He loves reading, golf, college basketball, and camping.

Kristen and Max have a son, Matthew. They also have a dog named Gracie, and two cats, Rhino and Mittens, who declined to be photographed.

Follow Kristen and Max on their blogs:

www.abeadnaprayer.com (Kristen)

www.wordwonderings.wordpress.com (Max)